THE

STORY OF A FAMOUS BOOK:

An Account

OF

DR. BENJAMIN FRANKLIN'S AUTOBIOGRAPHY.

BY

SAMUEL A. GREEN, M.D.

BOSTON:
FOR PRIVATE DISTRIBUTION.
1871.

CAMBRIDGE:
PRESS OF JOHN WILSON AND SON.

THE following article originally appeared in the "Atlantic Monthly" for February of this year, under the title of "The Story of a Famous Book." A small edition is now reprinted, with the consent of the publishers of that magazine, for a few friends of the writer.

1871.

THE STORY OF A FAMOUS BOOK.

It is now eighty years since the death of Dr. Franklin, and during this time his Autobiography has been more extensively read in this country than any other historical work. It was, perhaps, the earliest American book that acquired and sustained a great popularity. Other books may have had a greater local or temporary success, but to this one alone belonged a general and permanent reputation. There have been written many Lives of Washington, but none of them is to be compared in style and interest with the charming production of the great philosopher. Its history as a book has been so eventful, that it may be of sufficient interest to give some of its bibliographical details. The narrative was written at different times and places, and Franklin himself has given the circumstances under which he prepared it.

The first part, coming down to his marriage, in 1730, was written at Twyford, England, in 1771, while he was visiting the family of Dr. Jonathan Shepley, the Bishop of St. Asaph, with whom he was on terms of close intimacy and friendship. Franklin, as it might be expected from his inquiring mind, took a deep interest in the genealogy of his family, and while in England made a journey with his son for the purpose of finding out the history of his ancestors. The result of this trip is given in this portion of the memoirs of his life. The room in which it was written was afterwards known as "Dr. Franklin's room." The sketch was begun for the gratification of his own family, and intended for them alone, but afterwards it took a wider scope, and was evidently meant for publication. It was not until 1784 that he resumed work upon it, and in the mean time it had been shown to some of his friends. Three of them in particular — Benjamin Vaughan, Abel James, and M. Le Veillard — made strong appeals to him to go on with it. Mr. Vaughan's letter urging him to do so is dated January 31, 1783, and had considerable influence on his taking up again the story of his life, which he did the next year.

The second part of his memoirs, written while he was living at Passy, near Paris, is short, and made up mainly of his ideas on the philosophy of life, rather than the recital of events. When Franklin began the second part at Passy, he says that he did not have with him what had already been written. It might have been left at his home in Philadelphia after his return from England in 1775. This supposition seems plausible, for he would not have mentioned the fact if the manuscript had been lent temporarily to some friend or neighbor at Passy.

The third part was begun in August, 1788, while Franklin was at home in Philadelphia, and is brought down to 1757. This portion ends the Autobiography, as it is always printed, except in the edition of the Hon. John Bigelow, which we shall have occasion to notice before the close of this article. Franklin writes to Mr. Vaughan: "To shorten the work, as well as for other reasons, I omit all facts and transactions that may not have a tendency to benefit the young reader, by showing him, from my example, and my success in emerging from poverty and acquiring some degree of wealth, power, and reputation, the advantages of certain modes of conduct which I observed, and of avoiding the errors which were prejudicial to me."

At the end of Mr. Bigelow's edition is a fourth part, consisting of a few pages, written in 1789, and not to be found elsewhere in English. These are rather of a political character, and bring the memoirs down a year later, when they close. It was Franklin's intention, as may be inferred from his letters, to continue them further, and perhaps to the end of his life ; but during his last few years he suffered acutely. and much of the time was hardly in a condition to write for recreation or pleasure, to say nothing of his preoccupation with the public duties which pressed heavily upon him.

Immediately after Dr. Franklin's death, in 1790, the first portion of the memoirs was published in French, at Paris. It is a singular fact that this work, which was destined to have so great a popularity, should first see the light in a foreign land and in a foreign tongue. It has never been satisfactorily explained how or why this was so. It is not even certainly known who made the translation from the English into the French. It has been suggested that the translation might have been made from the copy which Franklin promised Mr. Vaughan, in a letter dated June 3, 1789. He there says that his grandson is copying the memoirs for his old friend. If this copy was sent, as is probable, although its existence is now unknown, it should have contained the whole memoirs, and the French version would have been full and complete. It has been said that M. Le Veillard was the translator, but he distinctly denies the statement, and furthermore declares that he is utterly ignorant of the manner in which the translator procured the copy. It is known that M. Le Veillard's copy contained the whole Autobiography, which makes it almost certain by circumstantial evidence that this was not the one from which the translation was made. According to the "Nouvelle Biographie Générale" (Paris, 1858), it was translated by Dr. Jaques Gibelin, who is spoken of in this dictionary as "a physician, naturalist, and French translator." He was an experienced translator of English, and moreover it is said that he had had the original manuscript in his possession. If this be true, it is very probable that he was the person who made it, and he may have used a copy which was obtained surreptitiously, although we have no knowledge of such a one. At any rate, a copy might easily have been made at any time between 1771, when the first part was written, and 1784, when the second part was begun, for we know that the manuscript had been shown to different persons, and some of Franklin's friends had read it. The translator, whoever he was, states in the Preface that he had a copy of the original manuscript in his possession, though he should not give the details — of no importance to his readers — how it came into his hands. This statement would rather imply either a slight irregularity in the manner of his obtaining it, which he did not wish to make known, or a complication of circumstances which it might not be easy to explain to his readers. He furthermore states that the portion in his possession only comprises the first part of Franklin's life, and this is all that was printed. The supposition seems fair that he made a copy, probably unknown to Franklin or perhaps forgotten by him. A note is added to the Preface of this French edition, requesting those who would like to read the Life of Franklin in English to send their names to the publisher, and that it would be put to press as soon as four hundred subscribers should be obtained. It is probable that this number was never secured, as the edition was never printed.

In 1793, two years after its publication in Paris, two separate and distinct translations of it were published in London, — the one by the Messrs. Robinson, and the other by Mr. J. Parsons. It seems a little strange that this should have been so, particularly as they appeared from the press about the same time. Perhaps a rivalry between two publishing firms, as sometimes happens in our days, was at the bottom of it. Probably the Robinsons' edition appeared first. Both were noticed in the "Monthly Review" for 1794 (Vol. XIII. p. 304). We are unable to give the names of the translators. The Robinsons' edition was edited with more care and is a better translation than the other. There is some slight reason for supposing that the editor had access to the original manuscript, possibly the one lent to Mr. Vaughan; though if this were so, it would be difficult to explain why he did not print the original draft, and the whole of it. Possibly the owner would not allow it. For instance, in the French version Franklin states that he sailed from Gravesend on the —— day of July, 1726, and arrived in Philadelphia on the —— day of October following. These blanks are correctly filled up in the edition of the Robinsons, with dates that agree with those in the original manuscript, while in Parsons's edition they are left unfilled. From this it would seem not improbable that the translator of the former had seen an original copy.

A few slight inaccuracies are also corrected, such as Sooper's Creek for Cooper's Creek, near Philadelphia, where Franklin passed a night with his companions on his first visit to the city. The translator of Parsons's edition speaks of a "school of natation," which is an expression that an Anglo-Saxon would hardly use. He also makes a singular blunder in calling one of the ballads that Franklin wrote in his boyhood the "Tragedy of Pharaoh." None would recognize under this title the little song which was known as "The Lighthouse Tragedy." The explanation of this droll mistake is found in the fact that the word for "lighthouse" used in the French copy was *Phare*.

The Robinsons' edition has been republished many times in this country and in England, and was the only one in either country, till Franklin's grandson, William Temple Franklin, published his grandfather's Works in London, the second volume in 1817, the first and third volumes in 1818. (The Life appeared in the first volume.) Even since 1818 the Robinsons' translation has passed through many editions, and has often been mistaken for the genuine Autobiography, though it was in a great measure superseded by the grandson's copy, which had the apparent stamp of authority.

It is, in fact, an English translation from a French translation of the original English. It has never to our knowledge fallen to the lot of any book to pass through such a series of changes as happened to this; and yet, with the drawback of these changes, it has been as charming as a novel to readers of all ages. Besides its fascination, it is full of that sound sense and practical wisdom which were so characteristic of its author.

Mr. Bigelow has fallen into a singular mistake, when he says that the Parsons edition is the one that has been republished, "not only in Europe, but in America, under the impression that it is both genuine and complete"; on the contrary, it is the only one that has never been reprinted in either country.

After the death of Franklin, his papers and manuscripts, including the original text of the memoirs, came into the possession of William Temple Franklin, then in Philadelphia, who began to arrange them and to prepare for their publication. To this end he wrote to M. Le Veillard, a few weeks afterwards, announcing the fact and requesting him to allow nobody to see the copy then in his hands, unless it should be the person who was to give the eulogy before the French Academy. A few months later he went to London, and there kept up a correspondence with M. Le Veillard about the preparation and publication of the memoirs. He was evidently apprehensive that an English edition would be published, as a French one and two English translations had already been, which would materially hurt the sale of the one on which he was engaged. From these letters to M. Le Veillard, it appears that there resulted a slight misunderstanding between them, which brought the correspondence to an end.

The preparation of the work which Franklin's grandson put forth in 1817 and 1818 attracted the attention of the literary world, and when it finally appeared it was received with great favor. It is destined, however, to yield to Mr. Bigelow's edition, which gives the *ipsissima verba* of Franklin.

The history of the manuscript is full of interest, and can be traced very closely. It seems that a copy of the memoirs was made in 1789, for M. Le Veillard, by Benjamin Franklin Bache, a grandson of Franklin, at that time a young man of twenty years of age. The copy was made partly at the instigation of M. Le Veillard, and was of course highly prized by him. It remained in his family — for he lost his life on the scaffold during the Revolution, in 1794 — during some years, when it was exchanged with William Temple Franklin, at his request, for the original manuscript, as he thought it would make a cleaner copy for the printer. In this way the autograph passed from the grandson's possession into the hands of a daughter of M. Le Veillard, and after her death, in 1834, it came into the possession of her cousin, M. de Senarmont, "whose grandson delivered it, on the 26th January, 1867, to Mr. John Bigelow, late Minister of the United States at Paris." It will now be understood how the copy made by Benjamin Franklin Bache passed back into the Franklin family, and furnished the draft for the printers of the first authorized edition. On a careful collation with this *editio princeps*, Mr. Bigelow finds that there are more than twelve hundred variations from the autograph text. Some of these, it is true, are slight and unimportant, but others are very material ones. It is possible that Franklin may have suggested some of them himself, while supervising the copy made by his young grandson, but the probability is that they were prompted wholly or mainly by the taste of William Temple Franklin. The language of the original consists of stronger expressions than the corrected copy, and in the greater use of colloquial terms. The statement of facts is also fuller, — entire phrases being sometimes left out of the copy, which might happen from the want of care in making it. But it is fair to put the burden of these changes on the shoulders of the editor of the work.

It is a fortunate circumstance for American literature that this valuable manuscript should have fallen into the hands of one who fully appreciated its value and importance, as Mr. Bigelow did. In 1868, the year after it was obtained, Mr. Bigelow published it, and this is the first and the only edition that has the stamp of authority. If one wishes to read the Autobiography of the philosopher in his own words, he must read this one. Mr. Bigelow has done his part of the work with care and discrimination, and has added some notes which throw light on the text, besides giving an interesting account of its eventful history. He has sometimes slipped into inaccurate statements, and in one place makes a suggestion which the context does not justify. On Franklin's first visit to London, whither he had gone on the representations of Sir William Keith, Governor of Pennsylvania, he had expected to take some letters of recommendation and a letter of credit for buying a press and types, but had been disappointed in receiving them either from the Governor in person or from his secretary. He was told that they should be put into the bag of letters that was to go on board of the ship. After reaching the English Channel, he got leave from the captain to search the bag for the desired documents, but without the expected result. He says: "I found *none* upon which my name was put as under my care. I picked out six or seven, that, by the handwriting, I thought might be the promised letters, especially as one of them was directed to Basket, the king's printer, and another to some stationer." In the first line of this quotation, Mr. Bigelow suggests that *some* was evidently intended instead of *none*, though there appears, as it seems to us, no reason for making the suggestion. Franklin undoubtedly meant what he wrote, and the sense is as complete as it would be with *some*. Moreover, the French edition of 1791 has given it as *none:* "Je n'en trouvai aucune sur laquelle mon nom fût écrit."

It is a curious fact in bibliographical history, that these memoirs should have been printed in English four different times, in four different texts, each one differing from the other in almost every line, thus making great and decided changes throughout the book. We give below the first two sentences of the Autobiography, as they appear in each of the four, though these are hardly fair specimens of the variations to be seen throughout the volumes, the differences often being greater:—

"My dear son, I have amused myself with some little anecdotes of my family. You may remember the inquiries I made, when you were with me in England, among such of my relatives as were then living; and the journey I undertook for that purpose."—*Robinsons' edition,* 1793.

"My dear son, I have lately amused myself with collecting

some little anecdotes concerning our family. You must remember the inquiries that I made among such of my relations as remained alive, when you were with me in England, as well as the journey I undertook for that purpose." — *Parsons's edition*, 1793.

" Dear son, I have ever had a pleasure in obtaining any little anecdotes of my ancestors. You may remember the inquiries I made among the remains of my relations, when you were with me in England, and the journey I undertook for that purpose." — *William T. Franklin's edition*, 1818.

" Dear son, I have ever had pleasure in obtaining any little anecdotes of my ancestors. You may remember the inquiries I made among the remains of my relations when you were with me in England, and the journey I undertook for that purpose." — *Mr. Bigelow's edition*, 1868.

It is also a curious fact in the history of this book, that there are no less than five editions in French, all distinct and different translations. The first one which has been spoken of appeared in 1791. This brought Franklin's life down to 1730, being that portion of the Autobiography which was written in 1771. The next edition was the one translated by Castéra, and published in 1798, with other papers of Franklin in two volumes. At the end of the second volume is given most of the second portion of the Autobiography. It seems singular that this was never printed in English until 1818. It was copied at Philadelphia from the manuscript which had been lent to Citizen Delessert. Perhaps the first portion of the Autobiography, about which there is so much obscurity, was copied in the same way after it had been lent to some friend. The Robinsons' edition was evidently used in the translation. The third edition in French, published anonymously, was taken from the London edition of 1818 (William T. Franklin's) and appeared the same year. This is attributed to Mr. Charles Malo. The fourth edition was that of M. Renouard, and was published in 1828. The translator had access to the original manuscript, then in the possession of the Le Veillard family, as he gives what we have called the fourth portion of the Autobiography, which appears in English in Mr. Bigelow's edition only. The fifth and last is the version of M. Laboulaye, which appeared in 1866, and followed Mr. Sparks's edition. These five editions were all published in Paris.

M. Laboulaye speaks of still another that was printed in Paris in 1841, which was "a new translation from the last edition published in New York." We have never seen this edition.

Those who have not read the Autobiography since their childhood we should advise to read it anew. It will be found to have charms that few books possess, besides giving an insight into the influences that shaped Franklin's character, and showing the motives that guided him through life. The book has passed through many editions among all civilized nations, and the demand for it still continues.

www.ingramcontent.com/pod-product-compliance
Lightning Source LLC
LaVergne TN
LVHW010834120826
845149LV00016B/1375

* 9 7 8 1 4 1 8 1 8 9 7 1 6 *